# A CULINARY JOURNEY

Exploring destinations and discovering different cultures and traditions is at the heart of every Viking journey. And of course food – not only the recipes prepared by our onboard chefs, but also local cuisine in all the fascinating places our ships visit – is an essential part of the overall Viking experience.

We hope this book helps you to recreate the flavors of your travels back home in your own kitchen, and inspires you to continue exploring the world.

# SCANDINAVIA & THE BALTIC

This region yields one of the most delicious, varied and healthy cuisines in the world, from the fjords of Norway to the rolling steppes of Russia. Many of Scandinavia's food traditions date back to the time of the Vikings, for whom the North Sea provided a rich supply of cod, mussels and salmon. Today, hearty dishes such as pork and meatballs contrast with exquisitely presented open sandwiches. The countries with shorelines along the Baltic Sea also rely heavily on fish, with an emphasis placed on soups and fish broths. The vast expanse of Russia ensures a diverse cuisine, with dumplings, potatoes and, of course, vodka, featuring prominently. Meanwhile, Iceland's culinary scene has evolved from humble beginnings to become an exciting, cosmopolitan scene.

# NORWAY

With its stunning mountains, wilderness
and coast, combined with an abundance
of fresh produce, Norwegian cuisine is
diverse, and usually quite unfussy, letting
the natural ingredients speak
for themselves.

# MAMSEN'S WAFFLES

**Serves 4–6**

8.8 oz (250g) all purpose
  (plain) flour
2 tbsp sugar
2 eggs
10 fl oz (300ml) milk
3 oz (90g) butter
Pinch ground cardamom
½ tsp vanilla extract

**1** In a bowl, mix together the flour, sugar, eggs and milk to make a smooth batter.

**2** In a small saucepan, gently melt the butter, then whisk into the batter along with the cardamom and vanilla.

**3** Cook with a Norwegian waffle iron or lightly oil a grill pan, heat to medium and cook 4-5 tablespoons of the mixture per waffle. Cook the waffle until bubbles start to form on the surface, then flip over and cook until both sides have turned golden brown.

# CHAIRMAN'S CHOICE: POACHED SALMON & CUCUMBER SALAD

**Serves 4**

4 salmon fillets
  (around 6 oz/170g)

**FOR THE CUCUMBER
SALAD:**
1 cucumber
Salt
2 tbsp sugar
3 ½ fl oz (100ml) water
8 ½ fl oz (250ml) rice
  wine vinegar

**FOR THE CHIVE SAUCE
(SANDEFJORD SMØR):**
1 pint (475ml) heavy
  (double) cream
2 ¾ oz (80g) butter
Salt and pepper
1 tbsp fresh chives

**1** Peel the cucumber and slice into discs. Sprinkle the discs with salt and allow them to marinate for 5 minutes. Pour away the excess liquid. Mix the sugar, water and vinegar, and cover the sliced cucumber. Place in the fridge for half an hour. Drain and reserve.

**2** Bring a pan of salted water to a boil, then turn down the heat and add the salmon fillets. Allow to poach for 8 minutes until the fish meat flakes.

**3** Meanwhile, prepare the chive sauce. Bring the cream to the boil in a saucepan, then reduce the heat and allow to simmer until reduced by half. Whisk in the butter, then add the fresh chives and season to taste.

(▶) Discover more at *exploringmore.com/video/salmon*

# RIBBE: ROASTED PORK BELLY

**Serves 4**

2.2 lb (1kg) pork belly
(rind on)
Salt and pepper
2 red onions
1 whole head of garlic
Thumb-sized piece of
ginger
2 bay leaves
Just over 2 pints (1 liter)
water

FOR THE CABBAGE
STEW:

8 slices streaky smoked
bacon
1 head cabbage
4 tbsp all purpose
(plain) flour
1 tbsp caraway seeds
4 fl oz (120ml) white
vinegar
1 ¾ oz (50g) granulated
sugar

FOR THE GRAVY:

3 ½ oz (100g) butter
3-4 tbsp all purpose
(plain) flour

**1** Preheat the oven to 425°F (220°C). Score
the skin of the pork belly diagonally to create a
diamond pattern. Season both sides of the meat.
**2** Quarter the red onions, half the garlic and
slice the ginger (no need to peel anything). Place
in the roasting pan with the bay leaves and top
with the seasoned meat, skin side down.
**3** Add the water and cover with foil. Turn the
heat to 350°F (175°C), cook for 1½ to 2 hours.
**4** Meanwhile, make the cabbage stew. Lay three
slices of bacon in the bottom of a large casserole
dish. Cover with a layer of shredded cabbage,
sprinkle with a light dusting of flour and a pinch
of caraway seeds, then season with salt and
pepper. Repeat the layering process to the top.
**5** Gently pour water into the pot until it's about
three-quarters full. Bring to the boil, then cook
for up to 1 hour, stirring occasionally, until the
cabbage is soft. Allow to cool slightly, then stir
in the vinegar. Add the sugar gradually to taste.
**6** Take the pork out of the oven and place onto a
rack skin side up, leaving some liquid in the pan
so that the meat doesn't dry out. Adjust oven to
425°F (220°C) and roast for 30 minutes until
the skin has started to puff up, then turn back
down to 350°F (175°C) and leave to roast for
a final hour. Move to a chopping board, cover
with foil and leave to rest.
**7** In a saucepan, melt the butter and add the
flour. Heat gently, stirring until it thickens. Add
the meat juices, bring to the boil and simmer for
a few minutes. Pour through a sieve and serve.

# LAMB FÅRIKÅL

**Serves 4–6**

2.2 lb (1kg) lamb
  shoulder
1 large green cabbage
2-3 tsp salt
15 black peppercorns
Around 1 pint (475ml)
  water

**1** Cut the lamb shoulder into slices around
1 inch thick (3cm). (If you would like to keep
the bone in, you can ask your butcher to slice
the lamb for you.)

**2** Cut the cabbage into quarters down to the
core, then cut each quarter into 3 or 4 wedges,
keeping part of the core on each segment to hold
the leaves together.

**3** Place a layer of lamb, then a layer of cabbage
into a heavy casserole dish, seasoning each
layer with salt and sprinkling over some of the
peppercorns. Repeat the layering process until
all the ingredients are used up, finishing with a
layer of cabbage.

**4** Pour over the water and bring to the boil. Turn
down the heat, then simmer gently for 2 to 3
hours until the lamb is very tender, occasionally
checking the water level to prevent the dish from
boiling dry.

# TROLLKREM

**Serves 4**

2 egg whites
6 tbsp lingonberry jam
1 tsp vanilla extract
1 tsp caster sugar

**TO GARNISH:**
Lingonberry jam

**1** Place all the ingredients into the bowl of a stand mixer (make sure the bowl is really clean).
**2** Whisk on the highest setting until the mousse increases in volume and forms soft peaks.
**3** Serve piled into individual glasses and garnish with some extra lingonberry jam.

# POTATO LEFSE

1 lb (450g) potatoes,
   peeled and roughly
   chopped into chunks
2.7 oz (75g) butter
2 tbsp double cream
½ tbsp salt
½ tbsp caster sugar
4.6 oz (130g) plain flour

1 In a medium saucepan, cover the potatoes with water and boil until tender. Place the potatoes in a large bowl and mash well. Beat the butter, cream, salt and sugar into the hot riced potatoes, then let cool to room temperature.

2 Stir the flour into the potato mixture. Pull off pieces of the dough and form into walnut-sized balls. Lightly flour a surface and roll out the lefse balls thinly (approx 2.5mm).

3 Cook in a hot griddle pan (or lightly oiled frying pan) until bubbles form and each side has browned. Place on a damp towel to cool slightly and then cover with the damp towel until ready to serve.

# SWEDEN

Swedish cuisine offers a range of tantalizing tastes. Cheeses, breads, meatballs (served with lingonberry jam) and potatoes are all popular. And whatever they're doing, the Swedes try to stop for a morning coffee and sweet roll in a tradtion known as *fika*.

# SWEDISH MEATBALLS

**Serves 4-6**

Olive oil

1 large white onion

1 lb (450g) minced beef

1 lb (450g) minced
  pork

3 oz (85g) panko
  breadcrumbs

2 eggs, separated

5 fl oz (150ml) milk

½ tsp allspice

½ tsp ground nutmeg

Salt and pepper

FOR THE GRAVY:

2 tbsp butter

2 tbsp all purpose
  (plain) flour

1 pint (475ml) chicken
  or veal stock

4 fl oz (120ml) heavy
  (double) cream

Parsley

**1** Heat one tablespoon of olive oil in a large frying pan. Finely chop the onion, then cook gently until translucent.

**2** In a large bowl, combine the minced beef, minced pork, breadcrumbs, egg yolks, milk, allspice, nutmeg and cooked onion. Season with salt and pepper. Mix well with clean hands, then roll the mixture into golf ball-sized meatballs.

**3** Add a further tablespoon of olive oil to the pan, then cook the meatballs in batches, taking care not to crowd the pan, until all sides are brown. Transfer to a plate.

**4** In a clean pan, melt the butter, then add the flour and whisk for one to two minutes until pale and bubbling. Add the stock slowly, whisking constantly. Bring to the boil, then turn down the heat and add the cream. Return the meatballs to the pan and cook for a further 10 minutes, stirring occasionally.

**5** Serve immediately with mashed or boiled potatoes, a spoonful of lingonberry jam, and a sprinkling of chopped parsley.

# VANILJKAKOR

**Makes around
24 cookies**

8 oz (225g) butter,
softened
2 ½ oz (70g)
confectioner's (icing)
sugar
1 egg, yolk only
1 tbsp vanilla extract
10 oz (285g) all purpose
(plain) flour (sifted)
Seedless raspberry jelly
(jam)

**1** Preheat the oven to 350°F (180°C).
**2** Cream together the butter and sugar.
**3** Beat in the egg yolk and vanilla, then add in
the sifted flour. Mix into a smooth dough.
**4** Take tablespoons of the dough and roll
between floured hands into small balls. Place on
a baking sheet lined with baking paper (not too
close together).
**5** Press a thumbprint into each cookie and
fill with a small amount of jam, then bake for
around 15 to 20 minutes until the cookies are a
pale golden brown.
**6** Decorate by sifting a little extra confectioner's
(icing) sugar over the baked cookies.

# DENMARK

Danish cuisine has its roots in its peasant traditions, with potatoes, rye bread, fish, bacon and sausages featuring heavily. Open sandwiches, topped with a cold cut of meat, pâté or cheese, are also popular.

# OPEN SANDWICHES (SMØRREBRØD)

**SALMON GRAVLAX ON RYE BREAD WITH MUSTARD DILL SAUCE**

**FOR THE SALMON GRAVLAX:**

3 tbsp salt

1 tbsp sugar

1 shot vodka

1 lemon, zested

1 tbsp fresh dill, chopped

1 salmon fillet with skin on, around 6 oz (170g)

**FOR THE OPEN SANDWICH:**

4 slices dark rye bread

Butter

Mixed salad leaves

**FOR THE SAUCE:**

3 tbsp Dijon mustard

1 tbsp honey

1 tbsp cider vinegar

1 tbsp olive oil

1 tbsp fresh dill, chopped

**1** For the salmon gravlax, mix the salt, sugar, vodka, lemon zest and dill together in a bowl. Place the salmon fillet on a shallow dish and cover completely with the marinade. Cover and refrigerate overnight under a slight press. Pour away the excess liquid the next day. Slice the fish thinly at an angle, beginning at the head end.

**2** To make the open sandwiches, lightly toast each slice of rye bread, then butter and top with salad leaves, and then thin slices of the sliced salmon gravlax.

**3** Mix all the mustard dill sauce ingredients together and drizzle over each sandwich. Garnish with fresh dill and a lemon wedge.

**ALTERNATIVE TOPPINGS**

Classic toppings include Danish blue cheese paired with tart raspberries and red currants, and beef carbonade: a seared beef patty served with an onion confit. Beef tartare is another favorite: raw, finely ground beef tenderloin is served with condiments including capers, chopped red onion, cornichons and a raw egg yolk.

▶ Discover more at *exploringmore.com/video/smorrebrod*

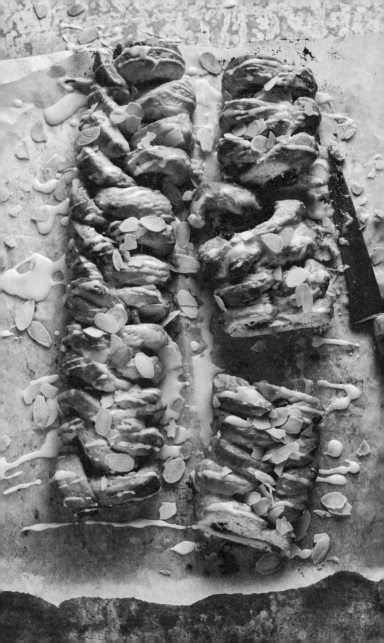

# WIENERBRØD - DANISH PASTRY BRAID

**Makes 2 braids**

4 fl oz (120ml) milk

0.25 oz (7g) sachet
dried yeast

9 oz (255g) all purpose
(plain) flour

6.5 oz (185g) butter,
chilled and cut into
¾ inch (2cm) cubes

2 tbsp superfine (caster)
sugar

1 egg, beaten

¼ tsp ground cardamom

Seedless raspberry jam

1 egg

FOR THE ICING:

4 ½ oz (125g)
confectioner's (icing)
sugar

1 tbsp boiling water

¼ tsp almond extract

TO GARNISH:

2 tbsp flaked almonds

**1** Gently warm the milk in a saucepan. Sprinkle over the yeast, then set aside for a few minutes.
**2** Using a food processor, mix the flour and butter until the butter is in small chunks.
**3** Stir the sugar, egg and cardamom into the milk mixture, then stir into the flour and butter. Bring them together into a dough and place in a clean bowl. Cover and refrigerate overnight.
**4** Flour the work surface and knead the dough briefly until smooth. Roll out into a rectangle around 16 x 10 inches (40 x 25cm). Fold the top third down and the bottom third up to overlap it, then rotate it by a quarter turn. Repeat the folds to make a very small rectangle. Turn and repeat twice, then refrigerate for 30 minutes.
**5** Preheat the oven to 400°F (200°C). Roll out again, aiming for 12 inches (30cm) by 14 inches (35cm) long, then slice into two lengthwise. Spread generously with raspberry jam.
**6** Cut about a third of the way in to the edges of each pastry, diagonally in about ¾ inch (2cm) thick strips. Fold the strips inwards over the jam, alternating between left and right.
**7** Place the finished pastries onto baking sheets lined with baking paper. Cover with damp kitchen paper and allow to puff up in a warm place for about 30 minutes.
**8** Egg wash, then bake for 18 to 20 minutes or until golden brown. Allow to cool.
**9** Mix up the icing, then drizzle over the pastries. Finally, scatter with the flaked almonds.

# BERRY JAM

2.2 lb (1kg) fresh berries
e.g. strawberries,
sliced
Juice of 1 lemon
2.2 lb (1kg) of sugar

**1** Put the fruit and lemon juice into a large pan. Heat for a few minutes to soften, then add the sugar and stir over a low heat until the sugar has dissolved.

**2** Once the sugar has dissolved and the liquid is clear, boil steadily for about six minutes, or until at setting point. To test if the jam is at setting point, spoon a little on to a cold plate, leave for a minute and then gently push it with your finger. If the jam separates without flooding back, setting point has been reached.

**3** Set aside to cool, then spoon into sterilized jars, label and seal with wax paper and lids.

# GINGERBREAD COOKIES

**FOR THE COOKIES:**

2 oz (55g) butter

2 ¾ oz (75g) soft
light brown sugar

2 tsp ground cinnamon

2 tsp ground ginger

½ tsp ground cardamom

1 tsp finely grated
orange zest

0.7 fl oz (20ml) of
clear honey

2-4 tbsp milk

8 oz (225g) plain flour

½ tsp bicarbonate
of soda

**FOR THE ICING:**

1 egg white

About 10 ½ oz (300g)
sifted confectioner's
(icing) sugar

Squeeze of lemon

**1** Cream the butter and sugar until light and fluffy. Add the spices, orange zest and honey and beat again, then add 2 tbsp of milk. Gradually add the flour and bicarbonate of soda and bring the dough together in a ball, adding more milk if necessary so it's not sticky. Wrap in plastic wrap and place in the fridge for an hour.

**2** Lightly flour your surface and roll out the dough ⅛in (3mm) thick. Use a cookie cutter to cut out hearts – if you want to hang them up, make a hole in the top. Gather the remaining dough into a ball, roll out again and keep cutting until it has all been used. Place in the fridge for 45 minutes and heat the oven to 350°F (175°C). Bake the biscuits for 12 minutes and allow to cool until hard.

**3** Make the icing and decorate. For a festive Scandi feel try writing 'God Jul' – Merry Christmas in Danish.

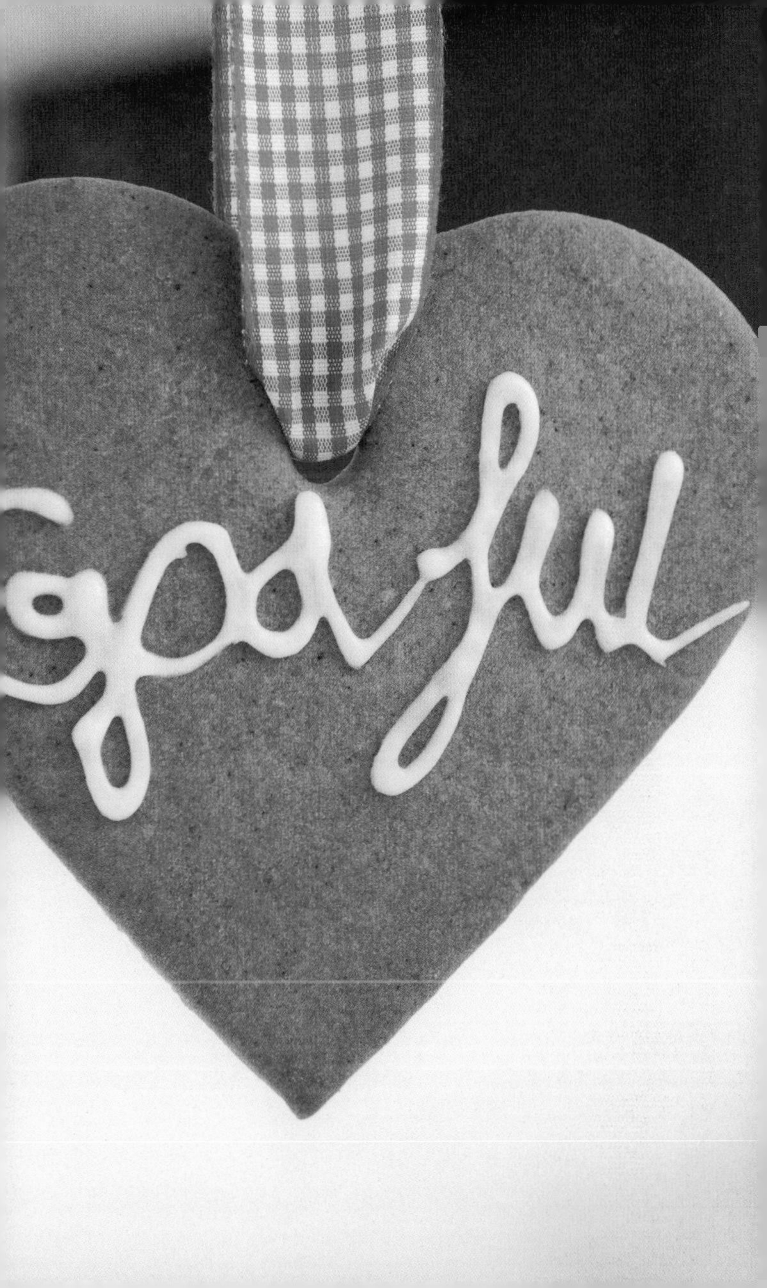

# FINLAND

Finland is known for its magnificent forests and lakes. Salmon and herring are staple foods, as well as deer and moose. Arctic wild berries, including cloudberries, are also popular.

# KORVAPUUSTI (CINNAMON AND CARDAMOM BUNS)

**Makes 15–20 rolls**

**FOR THE DOUGH:**

1 lb (450g) strong white
bread flour

2 tsp salt

2.5 oz (70g) sugar

1 x 7g sachet instant
dried yeast

2 tsp ground cardamom
(preferably freshly
ground)

5 fl oz (150ml) milk

5 fl oz (150ml) water

2 oz (55g) butter

**FOR THE FILLING:**

4 oz (115g) soft butter

6 tbsp sugar

1 tbsp cinnamon

**TO DECORATE:**

Pearl (nibbed) sugar

**1** Place the flour into a large bowl, then stir in the salt, sugar, dried yeast and cardamom.

**2** In a small saucepan, warm the milk, water and butter over a low heat until the butter has just melted, then turn off the heat and allow to cool to room temperature.

**3** Pour most of the milk mixture into the dry ingredients and stir with a knife until it forms a light, sticky dough. Reserve any leftover liquid for brushing over the buns before baking.

**4** Knead the dough in a food mixer or by hand for about 7 to 10 minutes until springy and soft. Leave in a warm place for about an hour or until it has doubled in size.

**5** Punch the dough down and roll out into a large rectangle shape. Mix the filling ingredients and spread across the dough, then roll tightly into a long cylinder. Cut the cylinder into slices around 2 inches (5cm) wide.

**6** Preheat the oven to 425°F (220°C). To create the shape, push down firmly through the center of each roll with an extended, flat index finger, pressing it down towards the base.

**7** Brush the rolls with the remaining milk mixture and sprinkle with pearl sugar. Bake for about 15 minutes or until golden brown.

# RUSSIA

Majestic imperial palaces, epic landscapes and its astonishing history make Russia absolutely unforgettable. Harsh winters mean that warming stews, soups and dumplings are all widely eaten, as well as blinis, little pancakes served with caviar, cheese and ham or jams and honey.

# BEEF STROGANOFF

**Serves 4**

1 ½ lb (680g) stewing
beef
Salt and pepper
4 oz (115g) butter
Small bunch scallions
(spring onions),
chopped
2 tbsp all purpose
(plain) flour
9 ½ fl oz (280ml) beef
stock
2 tsp Dijon mustard
6 oz (170g) sliced
mushrooms
5 fl oz (150ml) sour
cream, plus extra for
garnish
5 fl oz (150ml) white
wine

**1** Trim any excess fat or gristle from the meat.
Season generously with salt and pepper.
**2** Heat the butter in a large pan and add the
beef, frying until browned on all sides, then turn
the heat down and push the beef to one side of
the pan. Add the scallions (spring onions) and
cook slowly for around 5 minutes until softened.
**3** Sprinkle the flour over the meat and onions
and stir well, making sure the flour is completely
absorbed, then pour in the beef stock and bring
to the boil, stirring constantly.
**4** Lower the heat and stir in the mustard, then
cover and simmer for an hour or until the meat
is tender. Around 10 minutes before serving, stir
in the mushrooms, sour cream and white wine.
Season to taste and serve.

# BORSCHT

**Serves 4**

3 pints (1.4 liters)
  chicken stock
3 potatoes, peeled and
  chopped
½ a green cabbage, very
  finely shredded
3 tbsp olive oil
3 medium beetroots,
  peeled and chopped
1 red onion, finely
  chopped
3 tbsp tomato purée
2 bay leaves
1 lemon
3 tbsp chopped dill

TO GARNISH:
2 oz (55g) sour cream

**1** Heat the stock in a large pot and add the
potatoes. Bring to a simmer and cook for about
15 to 20 minutes until tender. Add the sliced
cabbage and cook for another five minutes.
**2** Meanwhile, heat the oil in a frying pan and
gently sauté the beetroot and red onion until
soft, then stir in the tomato purée. Transfer the
contents of the pan into the stock pot and stir
through, adding the bay leaves, a good squeeze
of lemon juice and two tablespoons of the
chopped dill.
**3** Season well with salt and pepper to taste and
simmer for a further 15 minutes. Serve garnished
with sour cream and the remaining dill.

# ICELAND

Iceland's isolated position has led to a long history of resourcefulness, and the country's simple diet is testament to this. Surrounded by the North Atlantic Ocean, fish is the mainstay of many dishes, but lamb and yoghurt-like *skyr* (technically a cheese) are also popular.

# PLOKKFISKUR (FISH STEW)

**Serves 4**

1 lb (450g) firm white
fish such as cod or
haddock
1 bay leaf
1 lb (450g) floury
potatoes
4 tbsp butter
1 large onion, peeled
and finely chopped
2 tbsp all purpose
(plain) flour
4 fl oz (120ml) milk
Salt and pepper

**1** Place the fish in a saucepan, pour over enough water to cover, then add in the bay leaf and a pinch of salt. Gently poach the fish until it starts to flake (about 8-10 minutes). Reserve the poaching liquid.

**2** Meanwhile, boil the potatoes whole with the skin on until tender. Run under cold water until cool enough to handle, then peel and roughly chop. Set aside.

**3** Melt the butter into the pan and add in the onion. Cook until softened and translucent. Stir in the flour and allow to cook for a few moments, stirring until smooth and bubbling.

**4** Measure out the milk in a jug and add the same amount of the fish cooking liquid.

**5** Little by little, add the liquid into the onion mixture, whisking and cooking until the mixture is thick and creamy. You may find you don't need all the liquid.

**6** Add the potatoes and the flaked fish into the sauce and stir gently. Season to taste and serve with generously buttered dark rye bread.

# KLEINUR (DOUGHNUTS)

**Makes around 30**

10 oz (285g) all purpose
  (plain) flour
3 tsp baking powder
1 tsp baking soda
3 ½ oz (100g) superfine
  (caster) sugar
1 tsp cardamom pods,
  seeds removed
Freshly grated nutmeg
2 oz (55g) cold butter
1 egg
7 oz (200g) thick
  Icelandic yogurt
Vegetable oil, for frying
Superfine (caster) sugar

1 Sift the flour, the baking powder and the baking soda into a large bowl, then stir in the sugar. Break open the green cardamom pods to release the seeds. Crush with a pestle and mortar, then add about ½ tsp of the crushed, fresh cardamom into the flour mixture. Add a light grating of fresh nutmeg.

2 Cut the butter into small cubes and carefully rub into the dry ingredients until the mixture resembles breadcrumbs.

3 Beat the egg and yogurt together until smooth, then stir into the dry ingredients. Knead into a soft dough then cover with plastic wrap and allow to rest in the refrigerator for 30 minutes.

4 Flour the work surface and roll the dough out quite thinly (about 4-6 mm). To shape the kleinur, first, cut the dough into strips of about 2 inches (5-6 cm) wide, then cut diagonally across the strips to form long diamond shapes. Cut a small slit in the center of each diamond and gently push the bottom point of the diamond through the slit, then pull down towards you to make a twist.

5 Half fill a large pan (or deep fat fryer) with the oil and allow to come up to 350°F (180°C).

6 Fry the kleinur a few at a time until golden, then flip and fry the other sides. Drain on kitchen paper and dust with extra sugar. Serve warm with coffee.

First published in Germany in 2018 by Viking

**Copyright © Viking**

ISBN 978-1-909968-35-6

Book design by The Chelsea Magazine Company Limited

Photography: James Murphy
Additional images: AWL Images, Getty Images, iStock, StockFood
Recipe testing: Rebecca Wiggins

Printed and bound in Germany by Mohn Media

**vikingcruises.com**